11176 words, 39 pages

WANDERERING SOULS

Short Stories By, Peter Olsson

Story #1

Elegy for a Librarian

Ryan Havens body was found in his small apartment a short distance from the Lane Memorial Library in Hampton New Hampshire. Ryan died a peaceful death from a carefully calculated dose of a barbiturate. He left a lengthy note… really an elegant memoir.

I was seven when the library and the world of books seduced me with wonder. Books contained my heroes, lovers, teachers and companions. Mom loved me and she loved books. Dad worked so hard at his two jobs that he said he didn't have time to read more than the newspaper. He dropped me off at the library on Saturdays before he went to work at his second job. The day he died at work he said as I got out of the car,

"Ryan, I'm proud that you love to read and do good at school."

The men near him when he collapsed of the fatal heart attack visited my mom and me. They said he grasped a picture of me and mom as he fell over his desk in his final moments. They said they knew how devoted to us he was. One of them said a prayer and we all shed tears.

Our priest helped mom find a job at the library. Father Kelly helped me get a scholarship to Fordham University. I never grew tired of all those hours in libraries around the friends, mentors and heroes I found in books. I was proud of my Master's degree in library science. Our beloved priest attended my graduation. I felt like father Kelly was my spiritual father.

I loved every day in my library work place until the mind-numbing monsters came. Eager kids and adults used to seek my help finding books. I enjoyed helping them find answers and a focus of their reading bliss in the pages between the book covers. I had no children so the kids I helped with term papers, school reports and reading assignments were special to me. Their smiles when a book really grabbed their interest pleased me no end.

Now come the mechanical monster machines and their internet. The cold world of the internet monster took my joy away. The gigantic instant worldwide reverberating source of easily found answers is like the ultimate narcotic. Kids rarely curl up with books in my library anymore. I get lonely. Kids don't ask me for help because they use the internet.

People do come to my library but to go on the internet computers. They all seem in such a hurry. Quick knowledge, sound bite news and views. Even TIME magazine has briefer and briefer condensed articles. Often on one page. At the downtown mall, I don't see kids faces. Only tops of their heads as they text endlessly like robots. I feel empty. Sad. Lonely.

The pleasant senior citizens used to sit for hours reading my library's collection of big print books. After my mom died they felt like my momentary moms and dads. I made special efforts to keep all good best seller books in large print additions for them. Now they most all stay home. They get large print Kindle machines. They order new books by e-mail. No books to hold and curl up with anymore. I miss their smiles and gratitude.

Out on the streets people walk along, heads down texting mundane thoughts to friends who also look down. I feel down because of their looking down. Won't they get neck problems? Very few look up to smile at me. I went to try to find father Kelly to talk to but was shocked to learn he died a month ago.

I am stunned. Now I can't even read. I try but somehow angry, lonely, resentful words fill my mind's pages. Words on pages all seem dark and shadowy now. I look-up barbiturate lethal doses. My mom had left some sleeping pills in her medicine cabinet when she died. Now I have a few glasses of red wine that remind me of holy communion. I feel soothed and envision my dad, father Kelly and my mom on the other side of my sadness. Now the pills provide my goodbye. I miss

my loving books.

Friends of the Lane Memorial Library were saddened at the news of Ryan Haven's death. A brief funeral was held. The new young parish priest and the library director stood looking down at Ryan's gravestone. The inscription reads. Ryan Havens 1980-2016 "He loved books".

Story #2

Peculiar Prince of Polls

Peter A. Olsson

Craig Cannon called them his work-related dreams. The exponentially repetitious dreamscape involved endless rows of offices in a huge building. Each office door had a *Help Wanted* sign. But, a frowny face surrounding the words. As soon as Craig entered the interview room the same things happened in rapid succession. The interviewer smiled broadly but said,

"We could love your work, but, your poll-taking doesn't meet our needs."

What the hell?... he thought again and again.

Office after office paved the meandering footsteps of his dreamscape's job searching. Democrat political offices, Republican offices, college and university PR offices, small and large businesses, drug companies, for-profit hospitals, not-for-profit hospitals, Planned Parenthood, financial investment services, big banks. Not one interviewer listened to his carefully prepared pitch as a basis for assessing his work. The interviewers had twisted shifting faces with many varieties of smirks, eye-rolls and phony grins. Like a perpetual twisted funhouse mirror.

He awoke once again from the dream sweating, angry and bitter.

Cannon was proud of his graduate study in political science. His professors complimented his clear and constant commitment to accuracy and truthfulness. He got an A+ on his master's thesis paper about over-sampling errors in poll-taking. Craig's core question to be answered was, do polls reflect the will, inclinations and true feelings of people polled? Or, did polls reflect the will, inclinations and purposes of the pollsters? Craig's answer, it depended on the sincerity and integrity of the pollster. Craig had started out excited in his chosen field of journalism and poll-taking.

Currently the only achievement he had to show for all his work was a crummy job working for a hick town newspaper in Mountain Grove Oregon. Cannon thought,

> *Damn it. I will do my phone polls at home at night. They will be so clear and fair. Big newspapers and magazines will come to love my work. I will be famous someday because of my honesty and truthfulness. I will be THE pol of polls.*

Craig wrote a letter each year to his sister on her birthday. This year he said,

> "Sis, no one really listens to other people. I have searched for just one person who really listens. You are the only one I've found that listens to me. That's why I write you every year. Our parents never listened. They were busy trying to tell us what to do,

what to believe, what was important to read, think

and do to be successful. Remember the poem I wrote

for you my senior year in high school?

Valued Listener (For Sis)

Special solace offered freely by a friend.

My soul's painful wounds soothed, healed.

To hear and be heard in exquisite depth.

Continuity of support a unique blessing;

Love as friendship, it's definitive statement,

Punctuated by your special presence.

Dad found my poem for you. He showed it to mom and

they sat me down to tell me that my poem was weird. I

should not do that again. "Find a girlfriend", dad said. I told

him you were a friend, a girl and my best friend. Dad rolled

his eyes like I was stupid, crazy or gross.

Sis my career is going bad. No employers like my

approach. Right now, I do adds for local businesses here

in Mountain Grove. My editor shows no interest in the polls

I suggest for the newspaper. The 2016 US elections

seems so important. Accurate polls seem so important for

America. My boss says we use AP and other big national

polls, not "Local yokels". He won't listen to my polling ideas and techniques. I get so discouraged Sis, I get thinking that people these days don't want sincerity, truthfulness or honesty. Or, they don't believe it is possible. They seem hurried, cynical and preferring sound bites.

I was so proud of my polling skills at Franklin Pierce University. I didn't just go through the poll questions mechanically. I tried to build some rapport with the person I polled over the phone. I figured the polled person would give me their true opinion if they felt listened to for a while. My professors liked my way of doing telephone polls. One of my profs said I do telephone polls like a kindly friend or trusted clergyperson. He said the sound of sincerity in a pollster's voice is a lubricant of the deeper domains of a polled person's true opinions.

I do phone polls each evening here in Mountain Grove and people seem to enjoy my listening to their ideas and concerns carefully. Often, they change their mind or opinion the more they feel listened to sincerely. Sis, I ask myself, "*What is sincerity? Trust?*"

Sis, these days I think constantly about Charm, charisma, trust and particularly sincerity. Why do some personalities possess the capacity to convey an aura of complete sincerity? They could be spell-binding in their ability to successfully convincingly project sincerity. I think that the lively trio of trust, (Charm, Charisma, and Sincerity), can be in the early lives of some future literary, political, business and religious personalities. Are such leaders seen as gifts from God? As actual gods? As convincing actors? Saviors? Many of these personalities had from infancy and early childhood had cute boyish or girlish grins. Tom Sawyer's grin and invitation to whitewash fences became an element of famous charm and sincere seduction. Shirley Temple's girlish grin and lively singing voice was impressive. Eye-brightness and an engaging self-deprecating sense of humor were also essential components of the trio of trust in leaders. A faint hint of a "Peck's Bad- Boyness" enhanced an individual's charm and charisma. It was enlivened by just enough rebellion and iconoclasm towards adult authority. If these traits went too far into a fast-talking glibness, as with Professor Henry Hill in *The Music Man*, sincerity faded into lack of audience trust.

Richard Nixon, Bill and Hillary Clinton, Robert McNamara and Barack Obama's speeches hovered on the borderline between the trio of trust and the purgatory of prevarication and obfuscation. Those five lovers of words and speechifying told lies shamelessly. Sis, truth and trust go together when it comes to assessing sincerity. Damn it sis, "Am I too sincere? Devoid of charm and charisma?"

Concerned about Craig as his sister Rose often was, she wrote a note of reassurance and invited him to visit on Christmas with she and her husband. Rose simply said,

"Craig, believe in your creative self, I do."

Buck Hayes is a short wiry balding fifty-year-old with a brusk old school journalist's façade. Wendy his long- time girlfriend and reporter at his paper said he had a heart of gold. But, it would take Denton Cooley the world- famous heart surgeon with Freud's help to find it. Buck, originally named Bromley, was dubbed Buck by his first boss at the Houston Chronicle. "Buck ", because he always bucked the prevailing tide. He had been the publisher and editor of the Mountain Grove Express for two decades.

Since the internet and social media were increasingly dominating print media, Buck had been sweating the paper's circulation figures for several years. Now suddenly subscriptions and circulation figures had soared. They were getting new subscriptions to the paper from all over the country in recent months. Though he enjoyed the sudden success, he wondered why? Buck asked Wendy to explore why because he had to know before hiring another reporter for the paper. Wendy was thorough as usual and came back from her assignment saying,

> "Boss, as she called Buck playfully, we have a Clark Kent helping us. I'm talking about quiet, mild- mannered Craig Cannon. That guy has been doing polls and surveys on his own time. Several times

when I was short on stories for my beat I asked Craig for material. He reluctantly gave me some but said you had discouraged him. New readers from all over the country and people locally are asking for more articles by Craig and stuff he talks to them about. They say when he calls on the phone they feel comfortable. One guy said,

'I really feel listened to. My opinion seems valuable to someone.'

Buck, this guy is dynamite for our circulation and profits."

Buck shook his head looking stunned. He took Craig out to lunch, pronto.

Craig Cannon got his first raise and promoted to a new department in the paper. His new by-lined section will be called, "Truth and Trust Territory", by Craig Cannon. Sister Rose and her husband enjoyed their free subscription to the Mountain Grove Express.

Story #3

ANOTHER SIDE OF BEAUTY

**DIALECTICS OF
WHOLENESS**
"Modern" Adam and Eve

Boys' insecure struggles, seek manhood.

Girls are waging brittle womanly wars.

Both struggles begin at soft breasts.

Cessation in earth, called Mother.

A cycle pervades all identity searching.

RAGE, serves to break away in rebellion.

POWER sought early externally, later
within.

DIGNITY, is found in mere
courage to search.

ENIGMAS, of separateness and oneness.

FREEDOM, is to risk a dark aloneness.

LIGHT found at the end of two long
tunnels.

A humbling process, is this whole becoming.

****

Marcia Mason was raped. Marcia had liked Luke a lot. She thought Luke was handsome, charming, thoughtful, and well-mannered. After their third date Marcia invited Luke to come in to her apartment for coffee before his long drive to his place. They had a good time talking and enjoying some light petting. Then Luke said,

"Marcia, I can't resist you. I want to make love to you tonight."

Marcia told Luke she liked him but didn't know him well enough. She said no. Luke grabbed Marcia and threw her on her living room sofa. He tore at her dress and began the rape moves. Marcia felt detached and numb. Suddenly her cozy living room became a surreal movie scene. Luke said,

"Your flirting and a teasing tells me you really want to enjoy fucking as much as I do. So, lay back and enjoy it babe. The more you fight the better it gets."

Finally, Luke zipped-up and left. Marcia was stunned, sore and then angry. Marcia began to sob thinking,

> *No one will believe me if I report him. That bee in Luke got out of control with his damn pollinating. I can't call anyone. Even my friends will say I cried rape.*

Marcia cried and cursed her way long into the night. She took several showers but never felt

clean. She shivered endlessly despite warm blanket and comforter.

****

Rape is physically, psychologically and spiritually painful. This is true for human beings at any age and of either sex. The physical pain, bleeding and soreness is jolting. Worse are the accusations and self-accusations. They call it, "blaming the victim". Self-blaming lingers on like the smell of fish after a long day of fishing and cleaning the fish. The very worst form of pain is the feeling that God or a good society's fabric has failed you. Because of your own poor judgment or inaccurate intuition, you have failed yourself. Shame lingers like a purple cloud around the rape victim for months, years.

****

Marcia's mom and dad.

Jane and Jack Mason worshipped their beautiful new baby girl. Jane named her Marcia after her mother who was a beauty queen. Jack agreed with the naming. Jane said,

> "Look Jack, Marcia's hair, eyes and face are perfect. She has both our good looks already."

Jack smiled and agreed. He also agreed that little Marcia was a beautiful duplicate of her deceased grandmother. Jack agreed again that Marcia would be a beauty someday soon and live happily ever after. Jack agreed that Marcia will look elegant in blue dresses. Jack was a maestro at agreeing. Jack always agreed with Jane. Things went better that way. Even a U.S. president feels better when everyone agrees with the infinite wisdom of his utopian policies. No uncomfortable follow-up questions please.

****

Marcia Mason was twenty- two today. She looked in the mirror thinking… *Today is mother's death day.*

Mother always said,

"Marcia Honey, your deep sky-blue eyes are a gift. They are magic jewels."

Mother always went on,

"Honey, you are just like me. We are both like rare beautiful flowers. All men long to pollinate us. Sometimes they swarm like hungry bees around us. Our beauty is a soft power that can get us the richest, most handsome and devoted males. Sweetie, always use your power well."

Marcia Mason loved her mother. Even more now that her mother is dead. Marcia thinks often how dead mothers are very much alive in their child's mind. Marcia often imagines a chatty conversation with her mother before a date or at a party where she might meet a dreamy man.

But, Marcia often secretly doubts her mother's pronouncements about their alleged twin-ship of beauty. Marcia is also ambivalent about her natural blonde hair and the curves of her body that boys and men, even old men, constantly notice. Those frequent looks by men contain a sly smile tinged by lust. Lusty looks linger in Marcia's mind like stale cigarette smoke. Men chatted- her- up with a real friendly style, but Marcia heard how they all were trying out their best pick-up lines. Those looks and lines made her feel vulnerable. Such attention disgusted her.

Marcia knew her face was the crowning factor that got her named the most attractive senior in her high school yearbook. A close girlfriend Karen Krause, said Marcia's perfect creamy fair skin and her high cheekbones were like her lovely naked boobs grafted onto her face. They shared a cynical laugh over that imagery. Good friends tell you their true thoughts…straight-up.

Marcia remembered how proud she felt briefly in her high school chemistry class with Mr. Walsh. Walsh said she had a good mind and hoped she would use it as a chemist or doctor someday. Walsh asked her to stop by his office after school so he could give her some catalogues about the good colleges she should consider. Marcia felt thrilled. Then when Walsh tried to hug her and kiss her, she felt stunned, then afraid, then angry. She shoved him away and ran.

Marcia still feels anger at Walsh. Disappointment and anger like that is cumulative. It festers like a chronic itching burning skin infection.

Lou Walsh 's salt and pepper beard reminded her of her daddy. Daddy died one month after mother. If daddy was still alive he would have hugged her and said,

> "No big deal Marcy, I'll have a talk with Mr. Walsh and principal Donaldson."

Marcia knew daddy would never talk to Walsh or Donaldson. He was too agreeable. Chemistry class became an ordeal after she rebuffed Walsh's pass. He would make fun of her in class when she didn't know an answer. Marcia swore Walsh graded her tests tougher and gave her a B- when she deserved an A in chemistry. Walsh quipped,

> "Marcia, blondes don't have more fun in chemistry. I hope I don't have to start telling blonde jokes about you."

That comment hurts. Other kids laughed. Marcia felt a strange mixture of embarrassment, anger and shame. Shame about what?

Marcia knew mom would say Walsh was just another bee around her flower. "Don't get up-tight about it", Marcia could hear her mother say.

Marcia thought,

Walsh is the jerk. He should be ashamed, not me.

Fortunately, the Krause family took Marcia in after her parents died. She and Karen became even closer. Like real sisters in an unreal world they joked.

Marcia found ways to feel strong and protected all by herself. She worked out with hand weights and learned Yoga and Karate alone with the help of videotapes. The Karate became valuable twice during high school dance dates. Those two creeps had acted all sweet, kind and considerate until they tried to force sex with her in their cars. One jerk named Ted had a black eye from where she popped him with a chop. Marcia never told either Karen or Karen's parents about the pushy boys. Marcia knew what her deceased parent's tepid responses would have been. Marcia envied her fiend Karen. Mr. Krause was tough and firm with boys who sought dates with Karen. Mr. Krause tried to be a good surrogate father for Marcia but he seemed to keep a distance from her. At least he didn't do a Walshian number on her.

****

Marcia had never told her parents that she planned to be pre-med in college. Mother talked endlessly how SMU would be a great place to meet a handsome guy with good prospects. Marcia laughed to herself about not wanting am MRS degree. The Krause's were pleased and encouraging about Marcia's decision to be premed and not pre-wed as she and Karen joked.

****

Premed was a breeze for Marcia Mason. For probably many reasons, Marcia had a good memory. She also found it a thrill to study anatomy with a total emotional calm and detachment. Marcia aced chemistry and Mary Sloan her chemistry prof told her she had great determination as well as a gift for thinking chemically. Dr. Sloan gave Marcia a glowing recommendation for medical school. Marcia couldn't wait to start her medical studies.

****

Medical school, medical internship and residency training is not like *Grey's Anatomy* on TV. Marcia thought,

> *The writers of that TV show must be sex-obsessed. Sex, pain and death are strange   bedfellows. But, not every fear, anxiety and triumph of a developing doctor requires an endless parade of celebratory orgasms.*

Marcia's med school classmates, professors and resident teachers did swarm like bees around her luscious flower. They all learned to keep a flirtatious but strictly playful friendly distance. One swarthy surgical resident doctor with tired but dreamy eyes tried to seduce her by saying that she was wasting her best sexy years. Marcia loved pediatrics and plunged into a private practice with all "her kids" as she was fond of saying.

Marcia particularly enjoyed counseling her "little daughters". Marcia quickly spotted particularly bright and talented kids in her practice. She took excellent care of all her patients but she put a little extra into encouraging the natural talents and abilities she spotted in her "kids". This good practice sometimes took special effort in counseling parents and confronting them about opening their eyes about their kid's genuine talents.

Marcia dated good-looking wealthy men. Some were colleagues and a few divorced fathers of her patients. She didn't have long term relationships with men. Some offered marriage but to no avail. Her office nurse was her old and dearest friend Karen Krause. Marcia and Karen often double-dated but Karen found no permanent relationship with a man.

 After fifty years of a dedicated life as a pediatrician, Marcia took the advice of her best friend and office nurse Karen Krause. In Karen's words,

> "We both are getting quite slow. We both have plenty of money. Let's retire while we have time to travel and enjoy life."

For several years Marcia volunteered to supervise and lecture medical students. Karen tenderly cared for her medically declining parents. Karen's parents died the same day. Karen and Marcia made their final days as comfortable as possible.

Then she and Karen settled into a high-quality retirement community. Their condo was a pleasant home base for respite from their travels and a place to entertain friends. If dementia invaded either of their lives, Riverview Heights had a cognitive support unit on the same grounds. Marcia and Karen became favorites of the Riverview Height's staff.

****

Karen Krause died rapidly from cancer. Marcia cared for her dear friend with tenderness and good humor. The staff were amazed how the two joked with each other even about Karen's disrupted bodily functions.

Two weeks after Karen died Marcia began to slip gradually into the relentless twilight of Alzheimer's disease. Marcia remained beautiful despite her eighty years. Tony, the only male nurse that Karen and Marcia had fully trusted and enjoyed said.

"Marcia stays perpetually beautiful like movie idol woman Julie Christy. Her blue eyes sparkle, especially when friend's kids visit and when she gazes at Karen's picture."

After a fall and bumped head Marcia began to decline rapidly. She would enjoy evening sunsets. Marcia would talk to herself in a chatty way as she looked fondly at pictures of Karen, her parents and Karen's parents. It was a late fall day. Moments before Marcia died, Karen said to Tony,

"The blossoms and bees are gone now."

Story #4

LUIS'S SANCTUARY

Luis wanted to be warm, happy, and able to smile. Like the people driving by the corner of Cezar Chavez and Congress Avenue, and nearby streets. It was a little sunny in Austin today, but December and now January have been cold. At night, Luis's two old wool blankets didn't keep him warm enough. At least the bugs were not bad so the grass and leaves near the freeway bridge helped with warmth.

"Wipe that crooked smile off your face kid! Get off my money spot Mex."

Damn, it was big Red! As the down-in- their- luckers called him. When Red said to get off his begging turf, you did it. If you didn't, Red would find you at the night camp areas later and beat you bloody. One night, Red kicked Luis as he slept. Luis had limped for weeks till the bruise went away.

 Luis thinks cold sweaty thoughts about something else,

> *Red is scary, but nothing compared to Victor. Thank God Victor hasn't*
>
> *come after me lately.*

Luis quickly moved away towards another street corner. The Austin cops basically looked the other way from "down-in-their luckers", unless they got into fights. If the luckers got too close to peoples' cars, the smiley people frowned. They get scared, and called in complaints on their car phones. The street rules for luckers in Austin had gotten simple, clear and rigid. Fights out on the street corners were taboo. Because fights and too aggressive begging meant no money from the smiley people in their shiny new cars. Victor's voice once boomed saying,

> "The smiley people in the shiny cars got to be treated really careful. Their damn guilt is a fragile thing. They got jobs and money but somehow know deep down, that a string of bad breaks could land them on our street or worse."

Victor said that someday soon even in rich Texas, more and more people would join the ranks of the down-in-their luckers. Especially hit would be those without a high school education or the new herds of pot smokers and other druggies. Victor said the government doesn't want to pay to feed potheads for years in their prisons anymore.

So, Victor cautioned further, saying,

> "When they give you money they are paying the big guilt-man… with a capital G. Don't scare em, but

don't look, act, or be so happy either. Damn, Luis, I

call it 'artful pitifulness'"

Then, Victor laughed his angry mocking laugh. Luis felt cold chills.

 He had hoped that by the end of the day he would have enough

money to afford a motel room where he could take a bath this week.

Then he could stop by St. Mary's and put a donation in the offering

box. Maybe even see Sister Laura. Her smile was like a tiny glimpse

of heaven. But, Luis just couldn't let Victor see him make an

offering or there would be literal hell to pay.

 Luis and scary Victor had gone to St. Mary's school together years

ago. Vic enjoyed beating up other boys after school. Sister Laura

stopped Vic from the fights when she could. Vic had hated Sister

Laura because he said she smiled too much. And, not at him.

Yesterday Luis had collected twelve dollars from the happy smiling

car people. Today, no luck, by late afternoon, Luis had received no

money and few car people were smiling or even looking at him. The

cold breeze bit into his face and through his tattered cloth jacket.

Red had stolen Luis's thicker warm fleece last spring. Red claimed that he had seen the jacket first in the ditch. The wet things started streaming down his cold checks and Luis started to cough and spit up those green and yellow gobs.

Luis feared what lay ahead. He was afraid the typical sequence was about to occur. First, the severe nervousness, then the body tension, and then the terrible confused crooked thinking. The crooked thoughts prevented him from finding the places he needed to go for protection. Then finally, came the need-fear dilemma of Victor's presence that earthquake voice. The voice Luis could feel, taste, smell, see, and touch. The power voice looked like a tornado made of whirling blood, spit and dust. It was the size of a pick- up truck that could run over him at dizzying speed. The voice smelled like puke and sweat with a taste like cooked garlic, hot sauce and onions

Luis's parents died in a car crash when he was twelve. Sister Laura knew Luis because she worked at the Catholic children's home and school. Luis as an only child with no known relatives had been sent to St. Mary's after his parents died. Sister Laura treated all the kids at St. Mary's home like they were her own children. She seemed especially kind and gentle to Luis.

Recently, Luis refused Sister's offer of the free shelter. Ever since Luis lost the church janitor job at St. Mary's several years ago, he felt too ashamed to accept charity. Especially from Sister Laura, who he had always loved.

Lucker camps in Austin are located under bridges, near isolated dry stream beds, and in dense underbrush at the sides of freeways near bridges. The shelter of the nearby bridges is essential in the event of rain or snow. Some luckers have plastic covers they use because trying to claim shelter under a bridge after a rain has started can lead to a beating from the lord of that turf. Luis and other luckers know they can't go to the camps to sleep until after it gets dark. This poses problems because in the near dark it gets hard to spot territories staked out by bullies like big Red. Settling in too close to Red's claim could result in a beating. If a guy or gal lucker had a bottle of booze or sometimes their body to share with Red, he might allow them to stay for the night in relative peace. It worked best if Red got real drunk and the lucker left Red's camp before day light.

Just before Luis got to the bridge area where he might find a place to put his bedroll and stuff down. Victor's voice boomed so loud that Luis's head vibrated. Victor said,

> "You sniveling bastard, no sleep for you tonight! I got a place for you but you got to walk a long way. See that parking lot of the H.I.B. Get one of those grocery carts to put your stuff in and listen to my directions sucker."

Luis did as he was told. Victor commanded Luis to keep walking along the service road beside US #35 south. He used an old towel to keep his hands warm as he walked all night. Luis's few possessions were not heavy except the sturdy fry pan he got years ago at a St. Mary's tag sale. It had come in handy one night when he drove off an angry drunken Red. Luis used to cook eggs or fish in it sometimes. Just before sun up, Luis nearing exhaustion and in a rare act of defiance, yelled,

> "Damn, Victor, where do you want me to go?"

Victor replied,

"Don't cuss me sucker lucker! {Loud long laugh.} A mile further, you will see a big strong building marked with a big sign with big red circles that look like that archery target at church camp. Even you can't miss it. Go in there, wash up and I'll talk at you later. Don't get in trouble punk."

Luis did as he was told. He left his grocery cart full of his things behind a dumpster outside the big red circle fortress. He only took his towel and toothbrush. The place had its own big red grocery carts. Luis took one to walk around with and placed his towel, soap and toothbrush in it. At six AM, there were only a few people in the place and none of them were smilers or luckers. One guy with a bright red shirt scowled and looked at Luis with suspicion. Luis wasn't scared because Victor had commanded him to be here.

Luis was amazed at this red circle friendly fortress. After he washed up in the restroom, he noticed that this place had all kinds of wonderful things for guests. There was milk, cereal, fruit and vegetables. Luis found a cereal bowl, a spoon and even some napkins. He took them to a chair in one of the isles. He enjoyed a good breakfast and then washed his bowl and spoon. He started exploring the rest of this special new place. He got a new toothbrush and toothpaste. Luis spotted a smooth warm new fleece jacket and put it in his cart. He smiled and said to himself,

"Eat your heart out Red!"

Then Luis put a long sharp carving knife in his cart. He might need it with guys like Red. The pistols and rifles were probably locked up somewhere. A twenty- two or bow and arrow would allow him to hunt squirrels or rabbits but he couldn't locate them. He placed a small tackle box, some fishing lures, hooks, bobbers and a fishing knife in his cart.

Luis moved leisurely toward the men's clothes section. A loud crying baby and her loud talking mother came towards him. Luis made a shushing gesture across his mouth with his index finger. Rather than being relieved and quiet, the women quickly hurried away toward the front door. Victor wasn't talking yet as Luis walked past an older couple looking at bath towels. They smiled at him until Luis gestured for them to be silent. Then they looked puzzled. If too much talking and too much smiling happened right now, Victor's voice would come blasting back in his ears and at everyone in this new place. Luis didn't want everyone in this nice place to be scared and confused like he was getting. He hated his jumbled thinking.

Suddenly Luis was frozen with fear. He got the cold sweats. That young man in the red shirt was coming towards him with two big policemen in front of him. Usually the cops looked the other way when they saw us luckers. The red shirted young man said,

"There he is officers. He is scaring customers."

Victor's voice boomed like on a public-address system in this place…

"Luis. You dumb ass! I told you to stay out of trouble. Now you got to cut and run."

Luis got even more confused. He knew he couldn't out-run the cops with his cart so he grabbed for the knife. The cops started shouting for him to drop it and put his hands on his head. Luis's thinking got real jumbled. Did the red shirted young man know big Red? Victor was saying nothing now. Victor had last told Luis to cut and run. Luis decided he had to cut his way out first, then, he could run fast with his new cart. As he moved toward the officers their guns went off with a huge roar. The bullets hit Luis's chest. A terrible pain struck him. Then as Luis's vision grew rapidly dim he had a last picture of his beloved Sister Laura. She had no smile, only a stark look of fear, then sadness just before the darkness.

A tearful Sister Laura was the only one attending Luis's graveside funeral. She said a prayer for Luis's recently departed soul and then reading a poem out loud.

LUIS

Hear a disheveled lovable man

of the restless street corners,

and shabby lives under bridges.

This frightened unsmiling city,

 blinded by the neon gloom

of endless allies soon forgotten.

Hear lonely souls unredeemed,

and homeless in the streets

DOING HAPLESS HARM: The Implosion of a Screwball Shrink

Peter A. Olsson

I will follow that system of regimen which, according to my ability and judgment, I consider for the benefit of my patients, and abstain from whatever is deleterious and mischievous. I will give no deadly medicine to any one if asked, nor suggest any such counsel; and in like manner I will not give to a woman a pessary to produce abortion. With purity and with holiness I will pass my life and practice my Art. I will not cut persons laboring under the stone, but will leave this to be done by men who are practitioners of this work. Into whatever houses I enter, I will go into them for the benefit of the sick, and will abstain from every voluntary act of mischief and corruption; and, further from the seduction of females or males, of freemen and slaves.

From the Hippocratic Corpus.

I was always a smelly screw-up. My mother loved me of course, but it was difficult. Mother overheard the newborn nursery nurses joke about Arnie Ames the monkey. Truthfully, mom said my cranky baby cry even resembled monkey sounds. My bowel movements were notorious in our house. They smelled worse than any of my brother's and sister's. My farts were my symphonies of sounds and smells. My dad told me I seemed to enjoy my abrupt stinky little farts. In fact, my first smile and laugh occurred simultaneously with what our Ames family began calling Arnie bombs.

[OK psychology students, go ahead, speculate about my future cursed anal fixation, (obstinacy, orderliness, maybe retentiveness,

stinginess, sloppiness, obsessive-compulsive diagnosis. But, maybe I will surprise you.]

My only social skills at day care were my patented Arnie bombs. The other kids saluted my efforts by booing and pinching their nostrils closed. Well prepared teachers had air freshener sprays handy. One classmate threw-up during one of my Arnie bombing events. Some parents complained.

[Despite their protests, I think people are fascinated as well as repulsed by farts. The vast variety of fart sounds and smells are an odd-ball symphony of revolting pleasures. Be honest. When social opportunity presents or privacy prevails…cutting-the-cheese or cutting loose a fart is a special pleasure.]

At summer camp after a good old weeny roast and baked beans, plenty of baked beans, I was the star of the campfire and bunkhouse. Except the poor kid in the lower bunk or others nearby. "Ah beans, the musical fruit, the more you eat the more you toot." Everyone in the bunkhouse giggled, even the counsellor named Rabbit Taylor. Every morning at revelry Rabbit made us all take our soap and jump in the cold lake. Once he threw me and my wet and soiled sleeping bag into the lake. My camper colleagues teased me about that for a week. I was an olfactory celebrity.

My boyhood fame was unique but a lonely one. I grew immune at being laughed at frequently. Better to be laughed at than to go completely unnoticed.

****

My medical school graduation ceremony was held indoors because of heavy rain. I liked that. Rather than fresh-smelling flowers and spring breezes, the musty lecture auditorium, stale bourbon, and perspiration smells dominated our indoor gowned ranks. My mom and dad wished I was headed for a surgery residency. Dad had said he could smell and taste the big money. My best clinical grades had been in gastroenterology's proctology section and my psychiatry rotations. I chose psychiatry because I felt superior and valued. Truthfully, I also always smelled better than any chronic psychiatry patient. My presence was now perpetually anointed by Brute after shave and Old Spice Swagger deodorant.

I was convinced psychiatry would be my profession when I got a high grade for a paper I wrote and presented to the department of psychiatry grand rounds meeting. The crowd of medical students, psychiatry residents and faculty laughed, chuckled and clapped after my talk. I felt joy that my colleagues laughed not only at me, which I was used to, but **with** me.

My presentation was on the topic of the psychological mechanism of **compensation** or over-compensation. I discussed Joseph Pujol who performed at the famous Moulin Rouge in Paris to capacity audiences in the 1890s under the stage name of Le Petomane (The Fart). Nobain and Caradec say Le Petomane had the remarkable ability to suck huge amounts of air into his colon, and expel it with such exquisite control that in passing flatus he could play musical tunes, imitate the staccato bark of a machine gun, or the roar of a cannon. He could blow out a candle at several feet. I was fascinated with Petomane.

[*I was wondering in secret if I could learn to perform the Flight of the Bumblebee with such methodology?*]

How did Le Petomane learn such control over colon and anal sphincter? He discovered it accidentally as a small boy. He was swimming in the ocean, after plunging from a rock ledge feet and butt first. To his horror he felt the rush of cold sea water distending his colon to the point of causing a severe colic such as one experiences when given an enema too rapidly by an over- zealous mother. Frightened, he rushed out of the water, only to find himself helplessly forced to expel large amounts of water from his anus soon after he reached the safety of the beach. Le Petomane's mother took him to their family doctor who recommended play on the beach but avoidance of the water.

Years later Le Petomane experimented further with the strange talent that his hind parts possessed. He found he could voluntarily inhale either air or water through his anus---and expel them at will. In time he perfected this capacity, and changed it from the frightening and freakish problem of his childhood to a talent which drew larger audiences at the Moulin Rouge than did the acting ability of Sarah Burnhart!

[It wasn't just the acclaim I gained from my paper that thrilled me about being a psychiatrist, there was a thrill about learning about patients' inner guts and ways of compensating.]

****

After psychiatry residency training I poured myself into building a practice. I wanted to get married but I didn't date much or spend time with relationships. My sex life took place exclusively when I was alone in the shower. I dated nurses because they admired my profession and income for a while, then after a couple of dates, not me so much. One nurse had the courage to tell me my sense- of-humor was weird. She had none but her eating disorder made her an inexpensive date.

[A good friend, one of my only real friends recommended that I get a psychoanalysis. I thought about it but felt I did not have the time. And, I thought I knew all I wanted to know about myself.]

My psychiatric practice went very well for several years. I built a reputation of being especially good at helping patients with gastrointestinal problems. I wasn't just good at prescribing the correct medications to help, I also spent long sessions listening to patients describing their bowel symptoms in vast detail. Many patients told their primary care docs how my patience, my soothing voice, and bedside manner helped them immensely.

[I affectionately called it my toilet- bowl-side manner.]

My practice stayed perpetually full. I realized that most doctors grew irritated and impatient with hearing patients go on and on about their, constipation, BMs, 'gas', loose stools, cramps, stomach aches, hemorrhoids, and especially their flatulence. Yeah, the wonderful spells of farting. I thoroughly enjoyed my work. I made good money. I kept copious and detailed notes. Doctors were glad to have me listen to these draining patients.

Then one day came Sheila. She was a tall willowy blonde with a full figure, beautiful blue eyes and that almost white blonde hair like Marilyn Monroe possessed. Sheila had every variety of bowel symptom which preoccupied her so much, she rarely smiled. When she did, my whole drab office seemed to light up like a beautiful sunrise. I often had rescue fantasies about my patients, particularly anxious preteenagers and dependent middle-aged women. But, Sheila slowly began to stir a new realm of rescue fantasy in me. I insisted on seeing her three times a week, then eventually four. Her wealthy oilman husband was fine with the considerable cost. With my special concerned listening Sheila did better and better. I so much wanted to see the glow of her smile.

Sheila shared more and more, especially her unhappy sex and marital life. Her husband preferred slam- bam- thank you- mam sex without any loving foreplay or tenderness. Sheila felt her husband was having an affair but he denied it. Her husband claimed to want anal sex and as Sheila felt better and better psychologically, she offered it to him. But he rejected her offers. As Sheila described these details I got intense erections and flushed with desire. She noticed my erection and at the end of a session, smiled, and reached out to fondle me. We embraced passionately. In my state of flooded desire, I asked to meet her at a motel at the end of the afternoon. She agreed and her smile warmed my soul with delight. I had found my love bomb.

As our torrid affair progressed I felt filled with happiness. I proposed that Sheila divorce her husband so we could marry. Sheila shocked me by announcing it would be impossible. Her husband's private detective provided pictures of us in bed. Sheila's husband's attorney filed a lawsuit against me and contacted the local medical society's ethics committee.

My practice went down the toilet. The malpractice insurance company wanted to settle the case quickly but I stubbornly refused. My records were so orderly and lengthy that lawyers spent hundreds of billable hours on the case. My colleagues on the ethics committee told me to my face that I was a disgusting mess. My lawyer said that he wouldn't clean up my mess. I fired him and withheld payment of his bill.

Sheila refused to see me or even talk over the phone. A colleague and friend told me that all Sheila's GI symptoms had returned with a vengeance. I did get a note from Sheila. It simply said:

"You stink Arnie! What a lovable screw-up."

[*I have been able to get a night shift as nursing assistant. I've come full circle back to BM and bedpans. My case has been disguised and published in the Journal of Medical Ethics. . Perhaps young future doctors can benefit from my messy case and the Hippocratic Corpus. "First, do no harm."*]

Story #6

AN ANCIENT FRIENDSHIP

The Bible's Old Testament says.

"After King Saul had finished his conversation with David, David

met Jonathan, the king's son, and there was an immediate bond of love between them. Jonathan swore to be his blood brother, and sealed the pact by giving him his robe, sword, and belt. King Saul now kept David at Jerusalem and wouldn't let him return home."

I   Samuel   18:   1-4,

(Tyndale, p243).

The Old Testament account of David and Jonathan's friendship is inspiring and instructive. In our "modern" world, few deep and lasting friendships exist between individuals, countries or their leaders. Jonathan and David have much to teach us about friendship.

We learn that just before David and Jonathan's special dawn of friendship, David had killed the giant Philistine, Goliath. Goliath had taunted and intimidated King Saul and his army, thus David became an Israelite hero after his triumphant defeat and beheading of Goliath. (Tyndale, p243).

Sensing David's burgeoning popularity, King Saul showed crafty political skill. Saul made David his special assistant and eventually commander of his troops. We soon learn that political affiliations like the one extended by Saul to David are shallow, and not akin to true friendship. The scripture tells us about a key event that occurred on the return trip homeward of the Israelite army, after David killed Goliath. Women had come out from every village to sing and dance in celebration for the King's victory. However, they sang this Saul-affronting refrain, "Saul has slain his thousands, and David his ten thousands". (I Samuel 18: verse 7). Tyndale, p243.

Saul's fragile narcissism was offended, and he became irrationally jealous of David. Saul was fearful that the people would want David to be king. Saul's mental state deteriorated further into psychotically depressed and paranoid ravings. David tried to soothe Saul by playing his harp as music therapy. Saul threw a spear at David trying to pin David to the wall. This happened twice and Saul schemed. He sent David into the most dangerous of battles so that David would be killed in combat. Eventually David fled for his life and hid in the fields. (Tyndale, p244-245). Rather than being concerned about the best leadership for and wellbeing of the next generation in Israel, Saul sunk into egoism and the selfish clutching of his personal power.

In contrast to his father, Jonathan had made a covenant of friendship with David:

"for he loved David as much as he loved himself". (I Samuel 20: 17. p246.) *

Stated correlatively, we are good friends, parents, spouses, citizens, and persons, in proportion to how genuinely loving and good we are to ourselves. This Old Testament 'Golden Idea' of I Samuel (above), (also Leviticus 19:18), is a morally majestic forerunner of Jesus Christ's New Testament 'Golden Rule'. (Matthew 19:19, Matthew 22:39, Mark12: 31&33, Luke10: 27, Romans13: 9, Galations5: 14, and James2:8).

Jonathan tried to talk to his father King Saul in David's defense. Saul said that Jonathan would never be King of Israel as long as David lived. Saul was trying to get Jonathan to betray his friend with this powerful inducement. Jonathan continued to defend his friend David to his father, the King. Saul became enraged at Jonathan, calling him a 'Son-of-a-Bitch'. (Tyndale, p246) When

Jonathan refused to collude in the murder of David, Saul threw a spear at Jonathan who stalked out angry and ashamed of his father.

Jonathan then warned his friend David by a secret pre-arranged signal, so David could flee to safety. David and Jonathan remained friends for life.

#7

PROFESSORIAL INCORRECTNESS

Peter A. Olsson

Sara Simmons said,

"Dr. Williams, I know I deserved an A not a B-."

Sara Simmons is a bright and pretty third year student. (*They used to call them juniors.*) Bryce Williams recognized Sara from other political science courses she had taken with him. Bryce didn't mind preparing and giving lectures but disliked office hours for students. They felt like a waste of time. After he completed his PHD Williams was eager to do research for books he planned to write… not deal with students' petty concerns and whining. Especially students griping about grades. Others, took up his time with answering

shallow questions that they could easily answer if they took careful

notes and read the textbook assignments.

Williams glanced at the term paper Sara handed him. Bryce kept his

professor's poker face. Really a practiced scowl.

Sara pressed further through his silence saying,

> "Dr. Williams, I covered every point from your
>
> lecture about the electoral college and even added
>
> points from Commager's text and my own ideas."

Williams liked to hear her say---Doctor Williams. And her anger

made her cuter.

Williams said,

> "Sara, perhaps it was your comment about how
>
> brilliant the founders were to form the electoral
>
> college. I probably reacted negatively because of my
>
> emphasis that the founding American fathers wrote
>
> and thought in a different time and era. They had no
>
> women members of their political club. Don't you

recall my starting a discussion about how the Bush v. Gore and Trump v. Clinton election results raised glaring public concerns about candidates winning by electoral votes while losing the popular vote? Sara, many new immigrant Americans might get confused about the democratic process in which they are trying to participate."

Sara asserted,

"But professor as the text and some of us pointed out. America is not a pure democracy. We are in a representative democracy which is protected by the electoral college. Immigrants to America best learn about the electoral college idea."

Now Williams was really getting annoyed. *Who does she think she is?! She asserts the obvious so cockily!*

Bryce spoke angrily now,

"Ms. Simmons, I had made very clear how valid the challenges Eric Holder and other contemporary legal

thinkers who favor abolishing of the electoral college
were for America. Especially in American subgroups
who feel more powerless than privileged American
white and established citizens. The founding white
male fathers could not have known how things would
change in America over many decades."

Sara did not back- off in deference, saying,

"Professor, I would argue that the founders thought
with sufficient depth and wisdom that their concepts
of government would, could and have allowed all
citizens to appreciate how the electoral college
protects the vote of all American communities large
and small. Candidates for office just can't merely
campaign in large population areas."

Williams felt threatened, stubborn. He could feel his face and neck
growing hot and red. He said as soothingly as he could muster,

"Sara, our faculty has discussed changes in our
teaching philosophy in recent years. In all liberal arts

classes, we don't want to merely present cold textbook material. We want you our students to consider nuances in understanding the emotional dynamics behind language, personal relationships, unconscious biases and prejudices in America. Certainly Sara, you have heard we your faculty talk about microaggressions towards black, native and Chicano Americans. White privilege and white power, particularly male power has accumulated in the emotional atmosphere in America over many decades. Even woman still possess less power. We feel that the American collective unconscious must be confronted, purged, and reconciled for America to be free of destructive prejudice and racial bias. Our college and university campuses must be a vanguard for progressive changes in America. This implies changes even to our legal and political systems."

Sara thought,

Oh my God. I feel over-powered in the very way

professor Williams is talking about this stuff. But, I

better just shut-up and listen. I can't believe this guy.

Williams felt relaxed and empowered now. He plodded on,

Such innocent kids like Sara have been raised in

religiously or socially stifling homes and

communities. Our mission is to help them loosen-up

their thinking. Expand their life horizons.

"Sara, our courageous supreme court justice Ruth-Bader Ginsberg has said that even Muslim Sharia law might need to be informing our American legal system as more Muslim immigrants join our citizenry. So even religious domains may need to be flexibly altered from the rigidity of the founding fathers.

We live in wonderful progressive times Sara. Even diversity and flexibility is required about young children who grow to feel that they were born in the wrong- sexed body. Or have core homosexual or bisexual identities. Our stereotypes about sex and gender need to be increasingly flexible Sara. The younger a child can be when gender reassignment surgery can be freely chosen, the less troubled their life will be. Could the puritanical founding fathers ever envision such legal changes?

Professor and student sat quietly for a while. Williams broke the silence,

"Sara, let's go get a cup of coffee".

Williams felt strangely satisfied with this student office hour. Sara said,

"No thank you professor Williams. I've got to go to the library. What have you decided about my grade?"

Bryce Williams PHD smirked and added a smarmy smile saying,

"Sara, you didn't hear me. Your grade won't be changed."

Outside the campus was gray and dark. Maybe a storm brewing.

#8

GOOD COPS

Pat Brady loves his wife Lori and his two kids, Billy five, and Sally three. Pat keeps a picture of them in the inner band of his uniform hat. Pat peeks at the picture every day before he starts his shift.

Pat's second love is his job. Ever since he was a kid in Brooklyn, Pat wanted to be a cop like his dad and his dad's best friend Chuck Colby. Pat's Grampa, Jake Brady, had walked a beat as a Brooklyn cop for 35 years till he retired. Grampa owned a small grocery store on Prospect Place until he died of a heart attack. When he was little Pat used to help Grampa at his store. When things weren't busy, Grampa would tell Pat fascinating stories about walking his beat. Grandpa loved to help people. Over a hundred people came to Grandpa Jake's funeral. Pat heard them talk about how he had helped them or even saved their life. Once, Pat asked Grandpa Jake if he ever shot anyone. Jake's face got super serious. He said,

"I only shot my service revolver once. It was the bad guy or me. That's all I'm ever going to say."

Then Grandpa quickly said Pat needed to do some sweeping for him to earn his candy money.

Pat's dad Mike Brady and Chuck Colby shared a squad car which was where their friendship began. Pat recalled sitting in rapt attention as his dad Mike and Chuck Colby shared war and peace stories about their job. On frequent Saturdays one or the other of the two cops grilled burgers and hot dogs in the back yard. Pat felt a total sense of boyish bliss at being allowed to be present during cop-talk. Chuck had two daughters Lorri, Pat's age, and Dolly the little princess. When the women and girls came out into the yard for food, the cop-talk shifted quickly to talk about both families' beloved New York Yankees, Rangers or Nicks. The moms looked worried if they heard the cop-talk.

Pat developed a crush on Lori Colby when he was nine. They even shared an embarrassed brief kiss when they celebrated their nine-year birthdays. Lori and Pat had July birthdays but he was a week older. Pat never let her forget his seniority. Pat and Lori dated frequently in high school and at their senior prom he proposed to her. Lori smiled a glowing yes. Pat would never forget that moment

Pat had already filled out his application for the police academy. They would have the wedding when he graduated the academy and Lori finished her LVN training. Lori volunteered at a nursing home where had a job waiting for her. The two cop families were joyful. They had steaks and champagne that Saturday rather than burgers and dogs.

The day before Pat's graduation from the police academy the horrible thing happened. Pat's mom Janet Brady's face grew ashen as she got the phone call from Chuck Colby at Brooklyn hospital. Mike Brady had been shot in the face. Janet and Pat drove as fast as possible to the hospital. They ran into the emergency room but Pat was dead. A priest had just given Mike his last rights and tried to comfort Janet who was sobbing uncontrollably. The priest was kind but his words floated off like little kids' soap bubbles into the antiseptic smell of the Brooklyn Hospital emergency room. Pat felt stunned, numb. He looked at his dad's body but the ghastly facial wound brought waves of nausea. That sight was etched in his brain for good. As Pat puked in a sink his tears began. Chuck Colby hugged Pat with his big burly arms. They cried together in that moment of no effective words.

Mike Brady's funeral at Saint Mary's was attended by many cops and their families. Chuck Colby spoke brief words, "Mike Brady was a fine man, a good cop, I loved him."

For Pat, the funeral service and wake were a blur of kind words and hugs. Lori's touch and hug helped him get through the day. Burgers and hot dogs were never the same. Chuck Colby helped Pat like he was his real dad. Chuck, Lori and Pat talked long into the next Saturday night. Chuck said Pat could decide not to be a cop. Chuck and Lori would understand. That surprised Pat but he sensed they both knew what his decision would be. Chuck was and is always more than a father-in-law. They became father and son of blue blood and the special friendship only cops know. Their family feeling was a unique form of the brotherhood and sisterhood of all cops.

Pat's graduation from the police academy was sad and solemn. Pat felt Mike Brady's presence and pride in a mystical way that would be with him for life.

After his first week at work Pat talked to the detectives on the murder case of his father. What did they have? Nothing. A retired guy saw the killing out of his second story window. Unfortunately, the old guy had bad eyesight and could only say the killer was a husky man about six feet wearing a dark hoody. Chuck Colby had been in a grocery store getting them coffees when he heard the shot and ran outside. The killer had fled from sight and Chuck was focused only on helping his partner Mike. The detectives said they would keep Pat informed. They never found the killer. Mike would often drive by that death spot. He found no clues. Only anger, sadness and questions only God could answer.

Pat drew a crusty veteran cop as his squad car partner. Sam Lewis is black and occasionally soliloquizes angrily. His topics are repetitive: Random killings of cops. Senseless, cruel, hate-filled. Sam said they were stirred- up and driven- on by bogus protests about police violence. The over- eager media reporters Sam says, are driven to get scoops about the exciting stories about cop killings. They were like sharks roaming the city waiting for tales and video of blood. Sam said even the president who had never ridden around with a cop on a Saturday night in Brooklyn or the Bronx talked his fancy words about cops needing better policing skills. The bumbling New York major echoed the same crap. Those fools even blamed guns when POTUS has constant protection by men and women with guns. Pat cringed when he and his partner Sam sipped coffee and donuts in their car during a break. Soo vulnerable, they were sitting like easy targets. And, they had no comfort of bullet proof glass because it would cost too much.

Sam though curmudgeonly, was as Pat gradually realized, protective probably over-protective of Pat. Chuck Colby told Pat that Sam had admired Mike Brady. The way Chuck could tell was how much Sam joshed with Mike with put-downs in the squad locker room. Sam's crusty style of overprotectiveness was annoying to Pat. It had a paradoxical effect. Pat felt ever more vigilant. Pat got jumpy, restless and fearful. As a young cop trying to be the best, Pat found nightshifts particularly bad. He tried to talk to Sam but he laughed it off as rookie nerves. Sam grew even more protective in a way that made Pat feel like a little kid. Sam gave him a bad time about gazing at his family pictures every time they got in their car at the beginning of the shift.

When off duty, Pat began to drink more beer than usual. Lori joked about his getting a beer gut if he continued. Pat seemed to have less joy in playing board games with Billy and Sally. Lori noticed. She told Pat she was worried. Pat asked the Sarge for a change of partner. Sarge told him to give it more time. He would talk to Sam. That made it worse. Sam grew increasingly sarcastic and pulled rank on Pat. He demanded that Pat get their coffee or lunches while he smoked in the car with the window open. Pat's anger was palpable.

Pat woke from the dream in a cold sweat, his heart racing and the sheets soaked. In his dream, he and Sam were chasing a robbery suspect down a maze of dark alleys. Sam kept yelling at Pat to run faster. Pat caught up to the perp. Pat yelled at the hooded fugitive to lie down. As Pat got his cuffs ready the perp turned suddenly. Pat froze. The criminal's face was bloody, torn apart and it was Sam Lewis in the Hoody!

Pat showered hoping the soothing water would help. He almost popped a beer at breakfast but thought better. Sam Lewis would be sure to smell it on his breath. Lori had that special worried look as he left for work.

Sam Lewis was in an ornery mood. As Pat glanced at his family's pictures in his hat band, Sam bitched about his ex-wife hitting him for money for his kid's birthday. Sam told Pat he was damn lucky because so many cops' marriages break apart. Pat had told Sam in the past how bad it was that he so seldom saw his young son. Sam suddenly stopped part way toward their territory at Bed Sty. "Large black and two donuts kid", Sam said. Pat cussed Sam under his breath as he went into the crowded coffee shop.

Pat heard the two pistol shots. BAM! BAM! He dropped the coffees and raced out the door. The husky kid turned from the car window toward Pat--- Pat could see Sam slumped over the wheel. The kid's face was shrouded by his hoody. Pat reached for his gun. The last thing Pat ever saw was that pistol aimed at his face. BAM!

It was a beautiful clear blue-skied day at Holy Cross Cemetery. Father Tom had said brief, kind but solemn words. Chuck Colby's big arms grasped Lori Brady on the right and the love of his life Ellie on the other. The twelve shots rung- out. The dressed blue clad cops snapped to attention as the police chief handed the flag to Lori. Tears

flowed. Little Billy and Sally sat in their Sunday best, looking

stunned and staring at the closed casket.